Joseph Smith

Karen Dixon Merrell
Illustrations by
Jerry Thompson

Brigham Young University Press, Provo, Utah 84602
© 1971 by Brigham Young University Press. All rights reserved
Second printing 1972
Third printing 1974
Printed in the United States of America
ISBN-0-8425-0953-4

1974   10M   2512

Before we were born, we lived with our Father in heaven. He loves us and wants us to be worthy to live with him again.

While we live on earth, Heavenly Father speaks to us through special men called prophets. They tell us what we need to do to live with him again.

Joseph Smith was one of these special prophets. He was chosen to be a prophet before he was born.

He was born in America, December 23, 1805, and lived on a farm with his family. His parents taught him to have faith and to believe in God.

There were many churches near the Smith home, but Joseph did not know which one was God's true church.

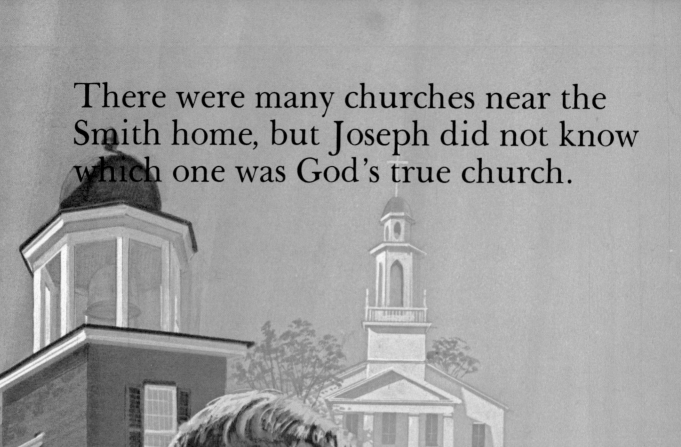

He read in the Bible that Heavenly
Father hears and answers prayers. He
knew that by praying he could learn
which church was true.

One beautiful spring morning, Joseph walked to a grove of trees near his home so that he could be alone to pray. As he prayed to ask which church to join, God the Father and his Son, Jesus Christ, appeared to him. Jesus told Joseph that the true church was not then on the earth and that he should join none of them.

Joseph told his family about what he had seen and heard, and they knew he was speaking the truth.

Later, an ancient prophet, Moroni, gave Joseph a record written on golden plates which had been buried in the Hill Cumorah near his home.

By the power of God, Joseph translated the Book of Mormon from these golden plates.

The Book of Mormon tells about Jesus and his visit to the people in America long ago.

Other important prophets of early days appeared to Joseph Smith. They taught him many things and gave him the priesthood so he could do Heavenly Father's work.

Joseph Smith helped restore Heavenly
Father's church to the earth once again.
This church is called The Church of
Jesus Christ of Latter-day Saints.

Twelve apostles were ordained and went with others throughout the world teaching people about the restored church. Many believed them and were baptized.

Joseph taught the people great truths which became new scriptures — the Pearl of Great Price and the Doctrine and Covenants.

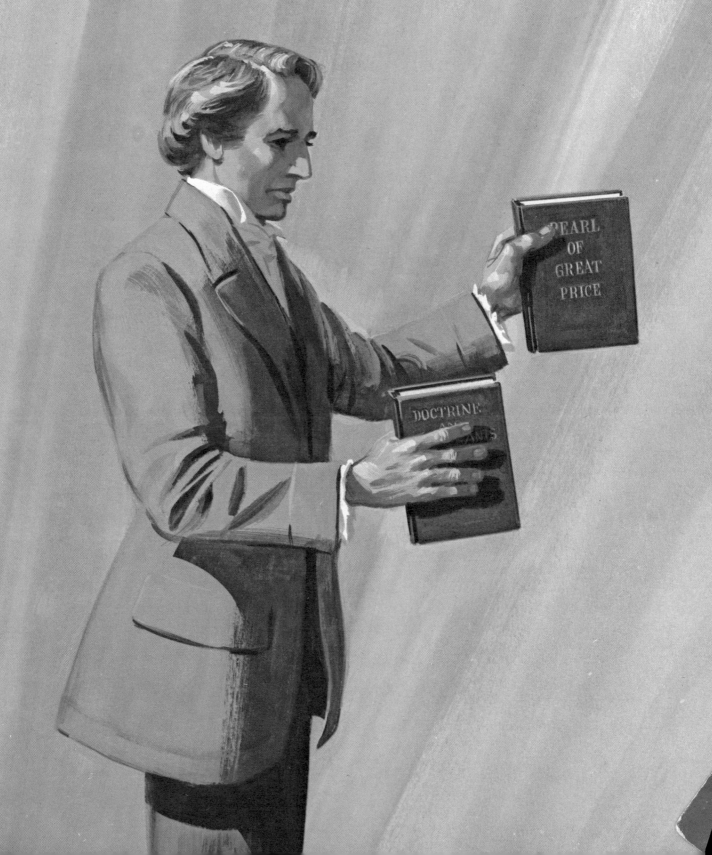

The Prophet Joseph Smith led the people as they built sacred temples and a new city.

Joseph was a friend to all who needed him. He helped the poor and healed the sick.

He enjoyed spending time at home with his family whenever he could.

Many people loved Joseph Smith and knew he was a prophet of God. Joseph restored God's kingdom to the earth. By his works he did more for us than any other man except Jesus Christ.

Some people did not believe Joseph was a prophet. He was put in jail many times and later lost his life.

After Joseph died, Heavenly Father chose other prophets to lead the Church. We are blessed to have a living prophet on the earth today.

We should thank Heavenly Father for sending us prophets. If we do what they say, we will be worthy to live with our Father in heaven again.